THE JEFF BLUMEN... SONGBOOK VOLUME 1

ISBN 0-9766625-0-7
First Edition printed June 2005 in USA
Overall design: Anna Kalinka
Cover Photography: John Ganun
Proofing: Tom Murray, Ted Sperling

For more information, visit www.jeffblumenkrantz.com

ACKNOWLEDGMENTS

This songbook is dedicated to

Hilda Levy, my Nana, who spent countless hours
and   at the piano playing four-hand duets with me

Nancy Blumenkrantz, my mother,
      who took me out of school to see Wednesday matinees.

Additionally, I would like to thank the following people and
organizations for their generosity, creativity, and inspiration:

Harold and Nancy Blumenkrantz, my parents,
whose love and support have made everything possible.

Victoria Clark, friend, colleague, teacher, and above all, Muse, who was
the first to sing many of these songs and helped "raise" them with me.

Audra McDonald, who put me on the map and continues to amaze me with her virtuosity.

Megan Mullally, whose collaboration, creativity, talent, and trust constantly inspire.

Lonny Price, whose belief in me has made such a difference.

Ted Sperling, who was one of the first people to notice that I could write.

My various collaborators: **Tina Howe, Annie Kessler, Aaron Latham, and Libby Saines,**
to whom I am ever grateful for their skill, generosity, and patience.

The BMI Workshop (Maury, Richard, Skip, Jean, et al), whose faith and feedback have
contributed invaluably to my development as a songwriter.

Beth Blickers, my agent, who said "yes" right away.

Anna Kalinka and John Ganun, who make everything look so good.

Tom Murray, who gave me a crash course in music prep and
whose sharp eye caught all my oversights. (I hope!)

And last but not least, those whose talent, love,
or support has touched these songs in some way:

Adinah Alexander, Farah Alvin, Susan Birkenhead, Jason Robert Brown, Carnegie Hall,
Matt Cavenaugh, Tracy Christensen, Jenn Colella, Bruce Coughlin, Colleen Fitzpatrick,
The Dramatists Guild, Harriet Golub, Marcy Heisler, Alison Hubbard, Alix Korey,
Judy Kuhn, Rebecca Luker, Sally Mayes, Chase Mishkin, Jon Wolfe Nelson,
The New Voices Collective, Casey Nicholaw, Nonesuch Records, Tracy Paladini, Ryan Perry,
Marcy Scott, Emily Skinner, the TMLP, Charlotte Vineburg, the WAA-MU Show,
Sally Wilfert, Michael Winther, and Maryrose Wood.

All Because of You

from *Urban Cowboy*, the musical

Music and Lyrics by
JEFF BLUMENKRANTZ

Do you see my hair?

Do you like what I done___ with my hair,___ Bud?   You can't

4

get your hands__ this red 'less you been wring-in' them__ all night. Well, I been

wring-in' and do-in' chores,__ pol-ish-in' sil-ver, scrub-bin' floors,__

wring-in', scrub-bin' all be-cause of you.__ Stay-in' up all night__

subito **p**

__ wait-in' on you__ gave me lots of time__ to think,__

sit-tin', knit-tin', star-in' at the tel-e-phone._____ And of all those thoughts,____

____ the on-ly one____ that gave____ me an-y peace____ was:

Thank the Lord I nev-er had kids____ of my own! Do you hear my voice?

Can you hear these words I'm say-in', Bud?____ I would-n't

f

have to say___ these words if you had picked up a phone___ and called. But now I'm

scream-in', and I'm tell-in' you dear:___ one more strike and you're out-a here!___

Try me! Test me! I swear it's true! 'Cause that's the

last night___ I'm pull-in', rub-bin', sit-tin', knit-tin', wring-in', scrub-bin',

8

stay-in' up through the night all be-cause of you.

Get it? Got it? Good!

Try me! Test me! I swear it's true! Yes, that's the

last night I'm pull-in', rub-bin', sit-tin', knit-tin', wring-in', scrub-bin',

subito *p*

Another Guy

from *Urban Cowboy*, the musical

Music and Lyrics by
JEFF BLUMENKRANTZ

Country/Folk feel ♩ = 128

Tom - my grabbed my heart with his stead - y gaze,—— and he swore his love for me in a

hun - dred ways, but he al - ways had to work a - round hol - i - days.—— Tom-

my was a bus - y man._____ One day I o - pened up his wal - let, saw his

State I. D._____ He was - n't twen - ty nine, he was for - ty three. That's where I

found that love - ly pic - ture of his fam - i - ly:_____ five kids and a wife___ named_____

___ Fran. It's just a - noth - er guy with an - oth - er lie,_____ an -

oth - er bro - ken heart and a good hard cry. I get up on my feet just as

fast as I can and keep on search-in' for a straight - shoot-in' cow - boy

man. Well, I fell for Fred-dy's cow - boy style, with his

rug - ged face____ and man - ly smile,____ and ev - 'ry - thing was per - fect for a

good long while____ 'til I no - ticed some - thin' was - n't right.____ Ya see, he'd

lin - ger in my bed - room when he got the chance,____ but there was lit - tle con - ver - sa - tion and no____

- ro - mance.____ Then I caught him pranc - in' round in my un - der - pants:____ Fred -

dy in my ted-dy, not___ a pret-ty sight. An-oth-er guy with an-

oth-er lie,___ an-oth-er sad sto-ry and a short-er cry.___ I

get up on my feet, just as fast as I can___ and keep on search-in' for my

straight - shoot-in' cow - boy___ man.___

With you and me, what you see is what you get.

As far as I'm con-cerned, that's the on - ly way to live.

But there are folks out there who just

don't care a - bout pre - tend - in' they're what they ain't...

and that's a crime too ug - ly to___ for-give.___ My

Poco meno mosso

dad-dy took off___ the day I turned thir-teen.___ Guess he could-n't han-dle the fa -

ther scene. He al-ways prom-ised me he'd be there as my go - be-tween,___

Tempo primo

but ob-vious-ly he lied.___ And now I won-der if I'm liv-in' that

his-to-ry____ with a string of liars____ from A____ to Z. Some-times I

doubt I'll find a guy out there as real as me,____ but you can't say I have-n't tried.____

And if there is a - noth-er guy with an - oth-er lie,____ an -

oth - er bad____ end - ing and a quick____ good - bye, I'll keep on get-tin' on my feet, just as

fast as I can_____ to beat the bush-es for my straight-shoot-in', truth - tell - in',

gen - u - ine cow - boy_____ man._____ I'll find my cow-boy man._____

Where's my cow - boy_____ man?_____

Departure

Music by
JEFF BLUMENKRANTZ

From a poem by
EDNA ST. VINCENT MILLAY

It's lit-tle I care what path I take, And where it leads it's lit-tle I care; But

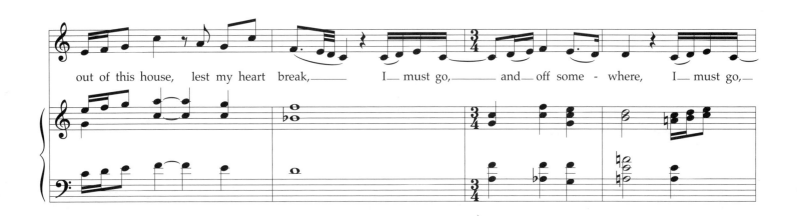

out of this house, lest my heart break, I must go, and off some-where, I must go,

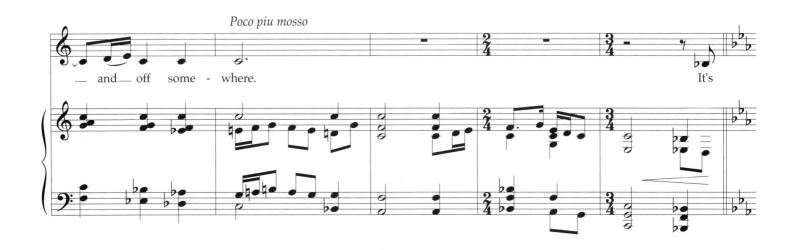

and off some-where. It's

lit - tle I know what's in my heart, What's in my mind it's lit - tle I know,____ But

there's____ that in me must up and start, And it's lit - tle I care____ where my feet____ go, And it's

lit - tle I care____ where my feet go.

Piu mosso ♩ = 84

I wish I could

walk for___ a___ day and a night,_____ And
find me at dawn___ in a___ des - o - late place_____
___ With nev - er the rut of___ a___ road___ in
sight,_____ Nor the roof of___ a house, nor the eyes___ of___ a face.___

where.

"Is some-thing the mat - ter, dear," she

said, "That you sit at your work so si - lent - ly?" "No, moth - er, no, 'twas a knot in my

thread. There goes the ket - tle,— I'll make the— tea."

Hold My Hand

Music and Lyrics by
JEFF BLUMENKRANTZ

some sweet fool____ who would dare____ to take____ my hand____ on a crowd - ed street,____ or at a

tab-le in some____ caf - é,_____ or e-ven half-way through____ a mat - i-nee.____

He'd some - times squeeze, and some - times stroke and some-times let it be._____ And

may - be I____ could trick that fool to fall in love_____ with

And when I find that chump who's will-ing to— em-brace my one— de-mand,— I'll

give the— moon, be -cause he held my hand.— My

strange - ly clam - my, chewed - up fin - ger-nailed, of - ten trem - bling, yet vir - tu - o - sic,

an - ti-bac - ter - i - al lo - tion-wear-ing hand.—

I Won't Mind

Music by
JEFF BLUMENKRANTZ

Lyrics by
ANNIE KESSLER and LIBBY SAINES

I won't mind sit-ting by your cra-dle, sing-ing to you soft-ly far in-to the night.

I won't mind play-ing peek-a-boo for ho-urs to

see that look of won-der, won-der and de-light. Soon they'll be ask-ing,

Con moto

"Where is Ba-by's nose? Where is Ba-by's shoe? Where is Ba-by's

hat? Clev-er lit-tle boy," they'll say. "Liz-zie taught him

that." I won't mind read-ing you a sto-ry,

poco rit. *a tempo* *Poco piu mosso* *poco accel.* *mf*

see your fa-ther lift you and swing you to his shoul-ders high a-bove my head.

Poco piu mosso

They may be bu - sy; I can take you skat-ing, I can take you sled-ding, fly - ing down the

hill. If they won't build a snow - man, Aunt-ie Liz-zie will.

They'll say, "Aunt-ie Liz-zie holds too tight," they'll say, "Aunt-ie Liz-zie can't let go," they'll say, "Aunt-ie

blank - et you with love as I hold you to my breast.

a tempo

rit.

Delicato, lento

Molto rubato

Liz - zie, he's not yours. Liz - zie, in his life your part is ve - ry

pp

small. But if one day a toy should break, or may - be play - ing pat - ty cake, you call me "Ma-ma"

colla voce

by mis - take, I won't mind at all._____

molto rit.

a tempo

rit.

I'm Free
from *Precious Little Jewel*

Music by
JEFF BLUMENKRANTZ

Lyrics by
LIBBY SAINES

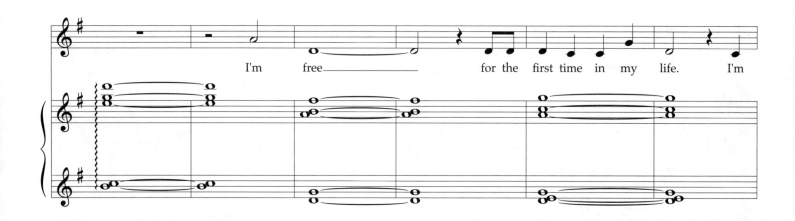

soul, free _____ and strong. _____ Oh

God, _____ let my life be long! _____

Independence Day

Music and Lyrics by
JEFF BLUMENKRANTZ

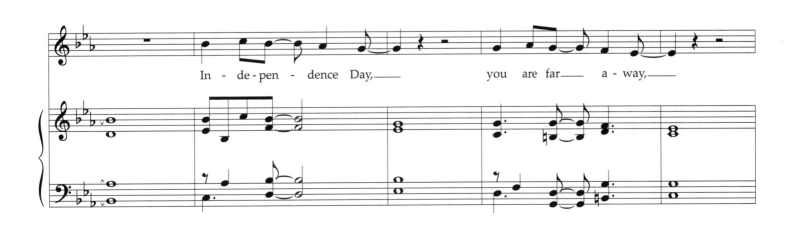

In - de - pen - dence Day,____ you are far____ a - way,____

far a - way____ from____ me.____ No - thing much____ to say.____

Piu mosso ♩= 124

Just a-no-ther day,___ wish-ing you___ could be___ here next to me,___

poco accel. *mf*

writ-ing___ more___ of___ our his-to-ry___ or

just en-joy-ing___ the hol-i-day.___ See the fire___ in___ the skies___

___match the fire___ in___ our eyes.___ *p*

It'll Work For You

Music and Lyrics by
JEFF BLUMENKRANTZ

O - kay. You say you're gay. (And I'd hate to think that I made you that

way.) But things don't have to be so black and white. I pre - fer a love - ly shade of

gray. We have a prob-lem, a ti - ny prob-lem, wreak-ing

ha - voc on my mas - ter plan. But don't you wor - ry— I've solved the

prob - lem with the help of mu - sic's great - est Jew - ish man.

Mar - ried with kids and boys on the side: the way I see it, that leaves ev' - ry - bod - y

sat - is - fied. If it worked for Leo - nard Bern - stein,___ then it could work for you.___

grand - kids! I did -n't raise_____ my on - ly son to leave me high and dry, with

no - thing to do. You'll give me grand - kids I can spoil as much as I spoiled you.

Len-ny knew best. Fol-low his lead. There'll be a time_____ to mess a-round,_____ but now's the

time_____ to breed. If the breed -ing worked for Len - ny,_____ then it - 'll work_____ for_____

you._____ Len - ny,_____ he

did his mo-ther proud._____ I want a Len-ny_____ so I can fin'-lly join the crowd_____ of kvell-ing

grand-mas with pic-tures for - ev - er on view. And if he's cute, I'll show a pho - to of your

boy - friend too. You know the plan. Heed it, my dear, and may - be

you'll start writ - ing mus - ic peo - ple wan-na hear. If kids in - spired___Leon - ard Bern - stein,___

they might in - spire_____ you.___ And you could write a *West Side Sto - ry!*___

It worked for Len - ny, God help me, it - 'll work for you.___

(spitting through her fingers)

Thpu! Thpu! Thpu!

ff

Lament

Music by
JEFF BLUMENKRANTZ

From a poem by
EDNA ST. VINCENT MILLAY

Lis-ten, chil-dren: your fath-er is dead. From his old

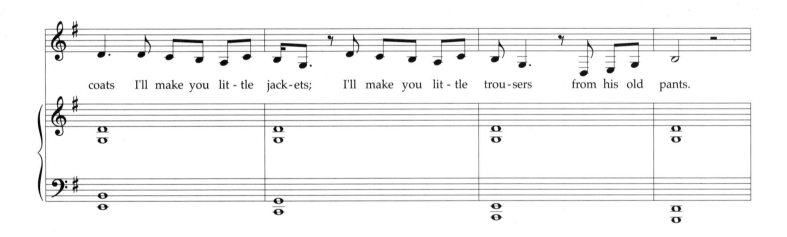

coats I'll make you lit-tle jack-ets; I'll make you lit-tle trou-sers from his old pants.

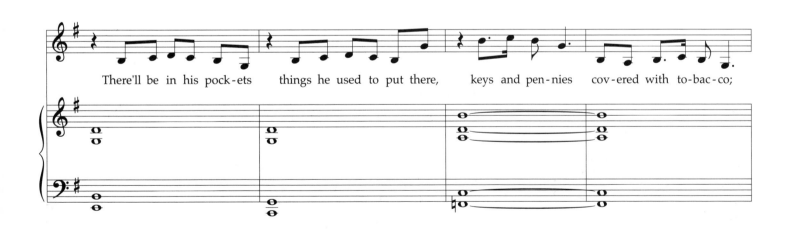

There'll be in his pock-ets things he used to put there, keys and pen-nies cov-ered with to-bac-co;

Love Is Not All

Music by
JEFF BLUMENKRANTZ

From a poem by
EDNA ST. VINCENT MILLAY

Love is not all:_____ it is not meat or drink___ nor slum-

ber nor a roof_____ a-gainst the rain;_____ Nor yet a

Love Is Not All - 4 - 1

Poco meno mosso, rubato

float-ing spar —— to men —— that sink —— and rise —— and sink —— and rise —— and sink a-gain;

mp

poco rit.

Tempo primo

Love can - not fill —— the thick - ened lung —— with breath, —— nor clean ——

mf *a tempo*

the blood, —— nor set —— the frac-tured bone; ——————— Yet

Poco meno mosso, rubato

man-y a man —— is mak - ing friends —— with death —— e - ven as —— I speak,

mp

driv - en___ to sell___ your love___ for peace,___ Or trade___

the mem' - ry of___ this night___ for food.___ It well___ may be.___

___ I do not think I would.___

Moving Right Along
(Part One)

(The text for a women's
version of this song can
be found on page 130.)

Music and Lyrics by
JEFF BLUMENKRANTZ

MAN 1: Ah, the freaks are out tonight.

MAN 2: Well, I've got to drum up three dates by Sunday, so we are going to sift through every guy in this bar until we find me a gem.

M1: Needle in a haystack.

M2: Creep-detector powered up?

M1: Check.

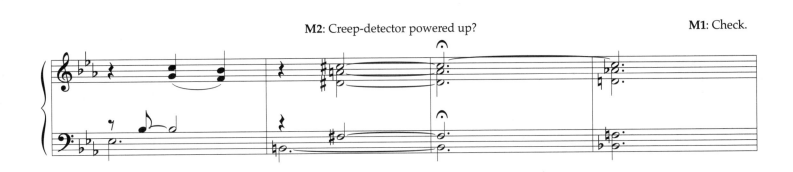

M2: Asshole-shield in place?

M1: Check.

M2: OK, I'm going in--

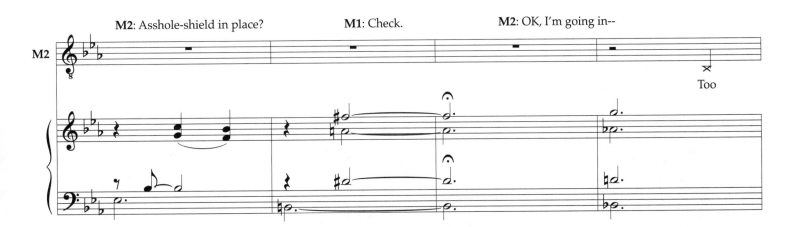

Too

64

Moving Right Along
(Part Two)

Music and Lyrics by
JEFF BLUMENKRANTZ

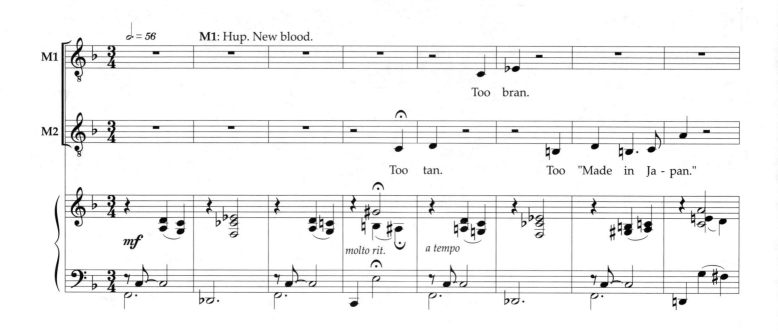

My Book

Music and Lyrics by
JEFF BLUMENKRANTZ

My ed - i - tor's a - bout to give up

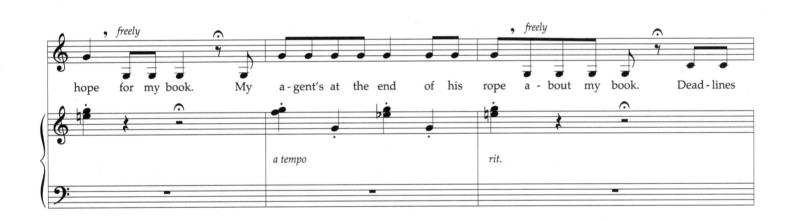

hope for my book. My a - gent's at the end of his rope a - bout my book. Dead - lines

came and dead - lines went, and my ad - vance is ful - ly spent, so I can't af - ford to sit a - round and

mope. Like a dope. A-bout my book. My___ big trans - gres-sion___

My name is Jody...

can be summed up in one pit - i - ful___ con - fes-sion:

...and I'm a slacker.

I've done everything in my power to avoid writing this book, but
I must be stopped!...Or started...and you're all going to help me.

If you hear an assignment that sounds
right for you, just raise your hand.

And please - don't be shy. I'm putting my
life in those hands...so RAISE THEM!

safety vamp

Some-one needs to wake me up at six ev'-ry day. Take the keys to my place, throw some

wa-ter in my face. If that does-n't work, then grab me by the hair, swing me

o-ver to my desk and chain me there. I may hate you,——

but I'll thank you in my book. I can't be trust-ed, I can't be trust-ed, 'cause if

it were up to me, I would stay in bed 'til three. I can't be trust-ed. I dis-ap-

pear! Which is why I called you trust - y peo - ple here.

Someone? Anyone?

Morning wake-up patrol? Do we have any takers?
(*Keep asking until someone volunteers.*)

Alright! That's very generous of you. We'll work out
the details later. OK, one down. Let's see…what else?

p

safety vamp

Oh yeah.

Some - one needs to come take my T - V real - ly soon! Bring a

mf

friend and a gun, steal the ca - ble box and run! Let me warn you: I will plead and I will

beg. Not to men - tion, I'll be cling-ing to your leg. I may hurt you, ——

but I'll thank you in my book. I can't be trust - ed, I can't be trust - ed, 'cause if

it were up to me, I would mar - ry my T - V. Are you dis - gust-ed? Most peo - ple

are... God on-ly knows how my ca - reer has come this far.

Anyone strong enough to carry my TV?

Anyone strong enough to carry my TV **and** kick me off at the same time?

p

safety vamp

(*Someone volunteers.*) Yes, you? Thank you! And good luck.

It's not as if I start my day in -

f

mf

tend-ing to shirk, yet shirk is what I do with shirk to spare.

O - thers are blessed___ with an ad - dic - tion to their work. Me? I'm ad - dict - ed to com -

pu - ter sol - i - taire!___

Oh oh! That reminds me! Someone needs to come over and delete every...

...**stupid, mind-sucking game** that has found its way onto my computer! Who's it going to be? Who knows how to do that?

(Someone volunteers.) Super! Wait, Mac or PC? *(They respond.)* Fab!   OK, I think I'm done!

1. safety repeat

2. last time

OK, I'm lying. There's one more thing.....   Oh God... this one really hurts!

Some-one needs to con-fis-cate my phones right a-way! Call and can - cel my plan, flush my

cell phone down the can. Once the deed is done, start run-ning for your life from the

har - py with the tur-key carv-ing knife. If I catch you,— I will

kill you,— but I'll thank you in my book. I can't be

shoot-ing you my most fer - o - cious look, that you're gon - na get a huge, em - phat - ic

"THANK YOU" in my Oh - my - God - I - can't - i - ma - gine -

ac - tual - ly - com - plet - ing - it - but - with - your - help - I - just - might - do - it book!

The Philosopher

Music by
JEFF BLUMENKRANTZ

From a poem by
EDNA ST. VINCENT MILLAY

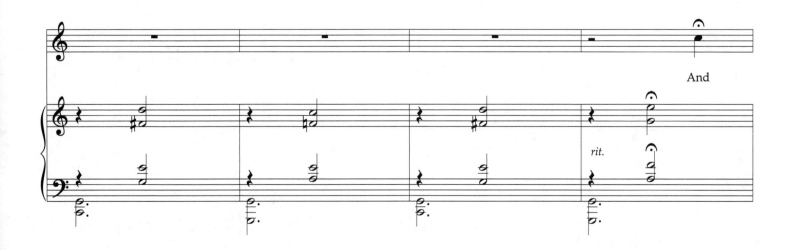

And

what are you that, want-ing you, I should be kept a-wake as man-y nights as there are

what are you, that you should be the one man in my

mind? Yet wom-en's ways are wit-less ways, as an-y sage will

tell,— And what am I that I should love so wise-ly and so

well?

Recuerdo

Music by
JEFF BLUMENKRANTZ

From a poem by
EDNA ST. VINCENT MILLAY

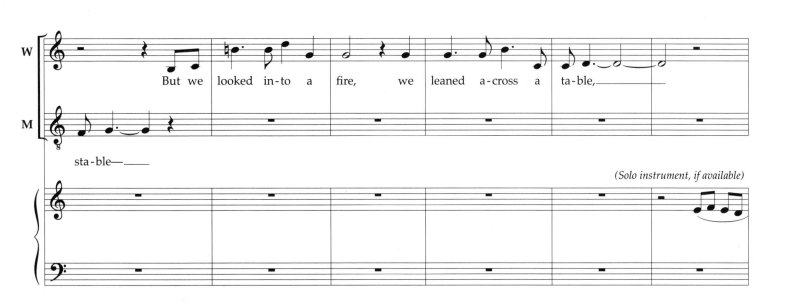

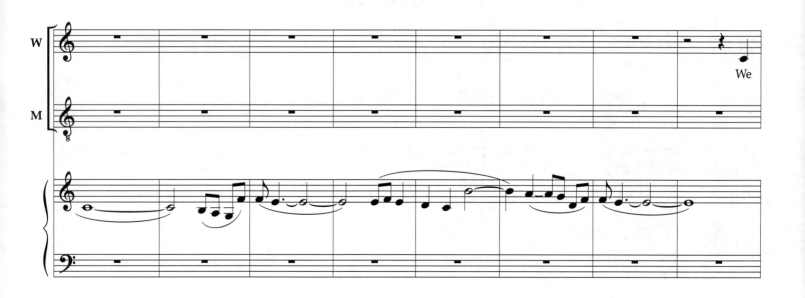

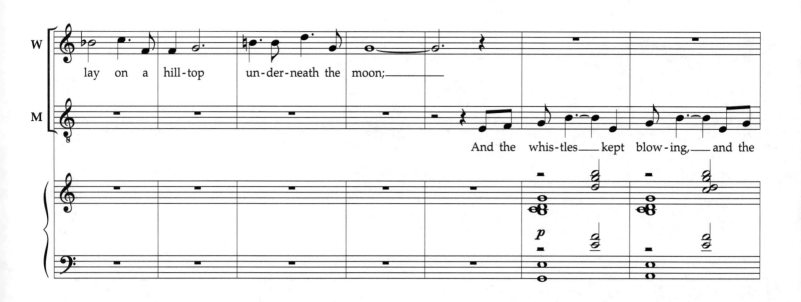

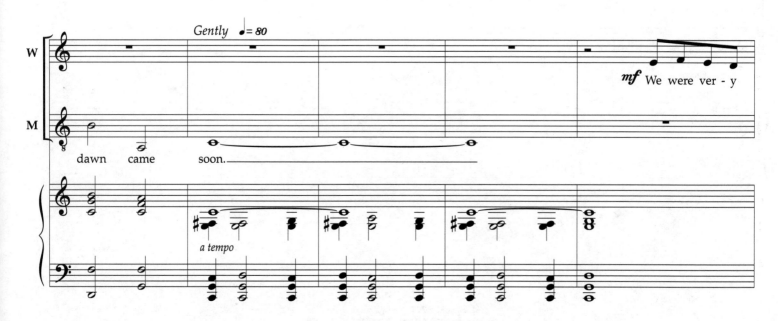

The Spring and the Fall

Music by
JEFF BLUMENKRANTZ

From a poem by
EDNA ST. VINCENT MILLAY

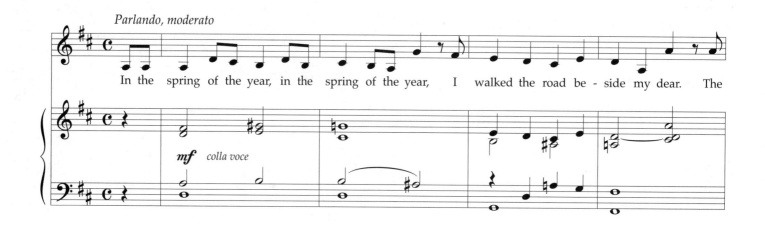

In the spring of the year, in the spring of the year, I walked the road be-side my dear. The

trees were black where the bark was wet, I see them yet, in the spring of the

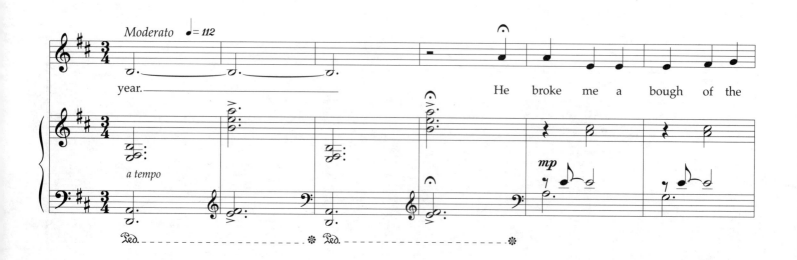

year. He broke me a bough of the

blos-som-ing peach that was out of the way and hard to reach.

Vigoroso ♩= 150

In the fall of the year, in the fall of the

year, I walked the road be - side my

dear. The rooks went up with a rau - cous

trill. I hear them still, in the fall of the year. He laughed at all I dared to praise, and broke my heart in lit-tle ways. ways.

Rubato, delicato, molto lento

bring out

Take the Filter Off

Music and Lyrics by
JEFF BLUMENKRANTZ

100

oth-er great guy! Why——should I set - tle—for dis - ap-point - ment when all I have to do to—

fly——   is take my fil - ter off?——

I re-mem-ber— my first—— time meet-ing you.

Oh yeah.——   My fil - ter start-ed shout-ing, and— it

set my mind to doubt-ing wheth-er you were the one____ to pur - sue.____

"He's way too at-tached to his mom. He's in-to Ed - na St. Vin - cent__ Mil -

lay. He's got a sen - si - tive stom - ach and__ the heart of a crit - ic, and I'm

kind - a sus - pi - cious he's_____ gay."_____ But

you took my hand___ and I nev - er looked back. We had a great year, and then you gave me the sack. If you

think I have re - grets, well I'm here to say___ that___ you're wrong,___ so, so___

___ wrong,___ I would -'ve missed out on a friend-ship I'll be treas - ur - ing my___ whole___

___ life long.___ I took the fil-ter off, I got a great boy-friend! Took the

filter off. So what? You ended up gay. Life's___ too precious for missed___ opportunities. I

never let one get away.___ I got my filter off.___

Look, we both know your filter has___ a

tendency to dominate. So_____ before___

filter off! It could be love at first sight. E - ve - ry day,— the Big— Gay Ap - ple is

off'r - ing you a— juic - y bite. So take the fil - ter off! My God,

he's a knock-out! Take the fil-ter off! What a re - mark-a-ble mind! Give— them more— than— a cur -

so - ry look. Don't— judge the cov - er, read— the damn book.— It's

time for your en - trance,___ and push has fin'-lly come to___ shove!___

Take___ the fil-ter___ off! Take___ the___ fil-ter___ off!___

Take___ the___ fil-ter___ off, and let your-self fall in

love!___

Time Does Not Bring Relief

Music by
JEFF BLUMENKRANTZ

From a poem by
EDNA ST. VINCENT MILLAY

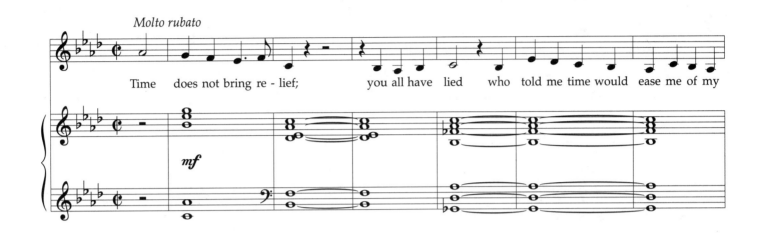

110

miss him in the weep - ing of the rain; I

want him at the shrink-ing of the tide; The

Piu mosso ♩ = *112*

old snows melt from ev' - ry moun-tain-side, and last year's leaves are

smoke in ev'-ry lane; but last year's bit-ter lov-ing must re -

broaden and cresc.

a tempo

Toll

Music and Lyrics by
JEFF BLUMENKRANTZ

sister Fran - ny mar - ried a guy from her of - fice, and Vic - ki's with a man whose house she

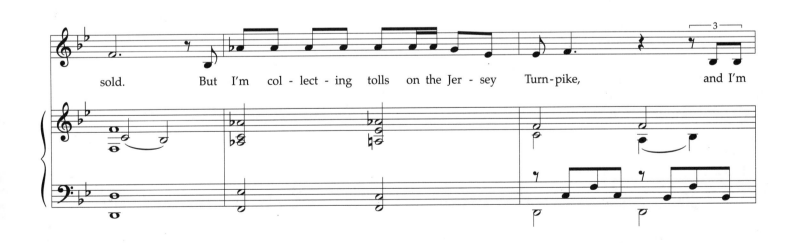

sold. But I'm col - lect - ing tolls on the Jer - sey Turn - pike, and I'm

start-ing to i-mag-ine my-self stay-ing sin-gle, grow-ing old. Lots of guys pass through, and you'd

poco rit. *a tempo*

think they could chat for a min-ute or two, but no! It's al-ways a rush with these

men. Yet there's this one I'd kill to see a-gain.

ten.

rit.

Moderato ♩= 116

Mon-day to Fri-day, he'd swing in-to my lane,___ my Tar-zan com-mut-er, for his change-

mf *a tempo*

mak-ing Jane.___ He'd give me a smile,___ like he wished he could stay, the

guy with the bean-ie in the blue Chev-ro - let. I

came to ex-pect him at eight for-ty two-ish. I'm not real-ly sure, but my boss___

___ thinks he's Jew-ish. He brought me a ba-gel one bliz-zard-y day,___ that

guy with the bean - ie   in the   blue Chev - ro - let.   To tell you the

Poco piu mosso

truth,_____ as he'd inch toward my booth,   my chest would start pound - ing and my

palms went damp,___ my legs got shak - y and be - gan to cramp.___ And

there he'd be   and all I could man - age to   say   was "Nave a hice

nee - dle - point bean - ie   and that   rat - tl - y blue___ Chev - ro - let.___

Why___ does my tongue get tied in a knot when I'm

faced   with a thing I want a lot?   Am I des - tined   to sab - o - tage my

dreams?___ Why___ did I

blow ev'-ry chance to con - fess? Was I wait-ing for him to just guess? Well, I

wait - ed too long, it seems, be - cause he

molto rit.

f

Poco piu mosso

went out and got him - self an E - Z Pass tag! Now he's whiz-zing by,____ and I've

a tempo

hit a big snag! "How can I reach you?" I hear my - self say to the

back of his bean-ie, pass-ing five lanes a - way. I could make an ap-

Poco piu mosso ♩ = 150

peal_____ to Of - fi - cer Neal to take me for a ride in his

subito **p**

Troop-er car_____ to find the blue Chev-y with the six-point star._____ We'd

chase him with the si - ren till he pulled a - side,_____ and I'd run to his win-dow all

hit a new low,___ chas-ing some guy whose name I don't___ e-ven know.___ But if you'd seen his smile,___

___ I'm sure you'd feel the same way_____ a-bout my guy with the bean-ie

in the blue Chev-ro - let. I know it's a cra-zy dream,___ but I'm gon-na find him some-

day._____

Walking the Wrong Way

Music by
JEF BLUMENKRANTZ

Lyrics by
LIBBY SAINES

At eight-een__ I was his wife, the on-ly man I'd ev-er known in my life__ un-til

you. And he'll be hurt. And you're so young. And this is wrong. How do I

get back to the world where I be - long? I'm

just can't seem to turn my-self a - round.

So man-y years in an end-less pa - rade. There for the laugh-ing and

there for the cry - ing. Milk-and-cook-ie years,_____ bed-time-sto-ry years...

When did love start dy - ing?_____ Ah____ but____

you, you bring me mu - sic and the sound is sweet. I see rain-bows___ in the

pud - dles on the ground.___ I'm walk-ing___ the wrong way down a

one - way street, and I just can't seem to turn my - self a -

round.___ Soon you'll be mov-ing a - way from my arms.

Moving Right Along

(Women's Version)

Revised Lyrics by
JEFF BLUMENKRANTZ

Part One

W1 Ah, the freaks are out tonight.

W2 Why do we do this to ourselves? Has anyone you know ever met a decent man in a bar?

W1 Has anyone you know ever met a decent man?

W2 Ouch.

W1 Look, think of it as a game. Besides, what else are we going to do on a (Saturday night in New York)*? Go to (some concert at Lincoln Center)*? Please….

W2 OK. You win….
Creep-Detector powered up?

W1 Check.

W2 Asshole-Shield in place?

W1 Check.

W2 Pepper spray?

W1 Oh yeah.

W2 Alright, I'm going in:

TOO THIN.

W1 NEXT.

W2 TOO OLD.

W1 CARRY ON.

W2 TOO CHIC.

W1 OUI.

W2 TOO…STIFF.

W1 Never too stiff…

W2 TOO SQUARE.
TOO FAIR.
TOO SELF-AWARE.
MOVING RIGHT ALONG…

W1 TOO JOWLY.
TOO SCOWLY.
TOO COLIN POWELL-Y.
MOVING RIGHT ALONG…

W2 TOO DUMB TO KNOW
WHAT NOT TO DO.

W1 TOO MUCH OF HIM TO HOLD ONTO.

W2 HE SMELLS LIKE CHICKEN VINDALOO.

W1 I SMELL EGG FOO YONG…

BOTH EW!
MOVING RIGHT ALONG.

W2 Want a drink?

W1 Cyanide and tonic, please.

TOO GRAY.
TOO FEY.
TOO BAD TOUPEE.

BOTH MOVING RIGHT ALONG…

W2 TOO DORKY.
TOO PORKY.
TOO NOT FROM NEW YORK-Y.

BOTH MOVING RIGHT ALONG…

W1 HIS HEAD'S TOO BIG
FOR HIS PUNY FRAME.

W2 HE LOOKS STRAIGHT OUT
OF A TOUR OF *MAME*.

W1 I'VE HEARD HIM BRAGGING;
HIS CLAIM TO FAME
IS A FILM CALLED *DONKEY DONG*.

W2 (Excited) Really??

W1 (Admonishing her)
MOVING RIGHT ALONG.

W2 Why??

W1   Don't go there.

W2   Why not??

W1   Starts with "V-" and ends with "-aginal rejuvenation surgery."

W2   Copy that.

        TOO CLEAN.

W1   TOO MEAN.

W2   TOO MUCH MAYBELLINE.

BOTH   MOVING RIGHT ALONG...

W1   TOO GRUMPY.

W2   TOO DUMPY.

W1   TOO FORREST GUMP-Y.

BOTH   MOVING RIGHT ALONG...

W2   HIS EYES ARE SWEET,
BUT HIS HAIR'S THE PITS.

W1   HE'S CUTE,
IF YOU CAN GET PAST THE ZITS.

W2   WHEN HE'S THE ONE
WITH THE BIGGER TITS...

W1   SURVEY SAYS: THAT'S WRONG!

BOTH   (buzzer sound) ANHHH!
MOVING RIGHT ALONG.

W1   Danger! Danger! Bad Toupee is heading right for you!

W2   Crap! What do I do? What do I do??

W1   Crisis averted. He's chatting up Blonde with Bad Extensions.

W2   Well, somehow that seems Karmically correct.

W1   TOO PALE.

W2   TOO MALE.

W1   TOO "I WENT TO YALE!"

BOTH   MOVING RIGHT ALONG...

W2   TOO FANCY.

W1   TOO DANCY.

W2   TOO DOCKERS PANTS-Y.

BOTH   MOVING RIGHT ALONG...

        EACH TIME WE COME,
IT'S THE SAME ROUTINE:
THE SAME OLD FACES,
THE SAME OLD SCENE.

W2   THE DORK,

W1   THE JERK,

BOTH   AND THE CLOSET QUEEN
ALWAYS GET THE GONG.
MOVING RIGHT ALONG!

Part Two

W1   Hup. New blood.

W2   TOO TAN.

W1   TOO BRAN.

W2   TOO MADE IN JAPAN.

BOTH   MOVING RIGHT "ARONG..."

W1   TOO QUIRKY.

W2   TOO PERKY.

W1   TOO CAPTAIN KIRK-Y.

BOTH   MOVING RIGHT ALONG...

        WE'RE OUT OF GUYS
AND WE'RE OUT OF LUCK.
OF COURSE, WE DON'T REALLY
GIVE A FUCK.
BETTER ALONE THAN
WITH SOME SCHMUCK.
THAT'S WHAT FRIENDS ARE FOR.

        THEY'RE FOR
BORROWING EARRINGS
AND TRIMMING YOUR BANGS
AND REMINDING YOU
YOU DESERVE MORE!

        THAT'S WHY WE'RE
MOVING RIGHT ALONG
OUT THE DOOR!

JEFF BLUMENKRANTZ began his career as an actor, performing in such Broadway shows as *Into the Woods* (1987), *Threepenny Opera* (1989), *Damn Yankees* (1994), *How to Succeed in Business...* (1995), and *A Class Act* (2001). Although he started composing as a teen and joined the BMI Musical Theatre Workshop in 1987, it was Audra McDonald's recording of his song "I Won't Mind" (lyrics by Annie Kessler and Libby Saines) in 2000 that launched his songwriting career. Since then, Jeff received a Best Original Score Tony® nomination for his songs in *Urban Cowboy*, the musical. His one-act pieces, *Woman with Pocketbook* and *Precious Little Jewel*, have been performed at several regional theatres, and he has been commissioned to write songs by Carnegie Hall and the Guggenheim's Works and Process program. Jeff is a recipient of the BMI Harrington Award and the Dramatists Guild Jonathan Larson Memorial Musical Theatre Fellowship. He is a graduate of Northwestern University.